100 Lessons That Will Change Your Mindset

Timeless Lessons on Discipline, Focus, and Thinking

Mindset Reading

Dedicated to Satguru Mata
Sudiksha Ji Maharaj

Introduction

Mindset Reading is a well-known book brand on social media. His book recommendations, reviews, and reading tips helped many peoples. Mindset Reading got over 600k+ followers across social media.

Reading books changed my life completely. Sharing learning's and recommendations of books have changed a lot of things. I received many messages about how my content inspired peoples to read books and become successful in life. I think this is the biggest achievement in my life to make changes in people's minds through non-fiction books.

Join the community!

Visit mindsetreading.com to learn more.

Check out our social media below:

Instagram: @mindsetreading

Twitter: @mindsetreading

YouTube: @mindsetreading

"You don't find passion, you build it. It is cultivated as you improve your skills. You get more passionate about something as you get better at it, and that something can be many different things throughout your life."

- Mark Manson

"You don't have to be great to start, but you have to start to be great."

- Zig Ziglar

"Sleep for 8 hours, not 6. Read for 2 hours not 4. Exercise for 1 hour, not 4 Deep work for 4 hours, not 10.

You are a human, not a machine."

- Will Goto

"A man is great not because he hasn't failed; a man is great because failure hasn't stopped him."

- Confucius

"Two things are infinite: the universe and human stupidity; and I'm not sure about the universe."

- Albert Einstein

"If you don't know, the thing to do is not to get scared, but to learn."

- Ayn Rand

"Most people don't know why they're doing what they're doing. They imitate others, go with the flow, and follow paths without making their own."

- Derek Sivers

"Once your mindset changes, everything on the outside will change along with it."

- Steve Maraboli

"The safest way to get what you want is to deserve what you want."

- Charlie T. Munger

"The person you marry is the person you fight with.

The house you buy is the house you repair.

The dream job you take is the job you stress over.

Everything comes with an inherent sacrifice, whatever makes us feel good will also inevitably make us feel bad."

- Mark Manson

"I always tell people if you want to know the secret to happiness, I can give it to you in one word: progress. Progress equals happiness."

- Tony Robbins

"If everything around seems dark, look again, you may be the light."

- Rumi

"The magic you're looking for is in the work you're avoiding."

\- Chris Williamson

"Thinking is difficult, that's why most people judge."

- Carl Jung

"The world as we have created it is a process of our thinking. It cannot be changed without changing our thinking."

- Albert Einstein

"**Never hold yourself back from trying something new just because you're afraid you won't be good enough.**

You'll never get the opportunity to do your best work if you're not willing to first do your worst and then let yourself learn and grow."

- Lori Deschene

"Nothing exists except atoms and empty space; everything else is opinion."

- Democritus

"Who you are, what you think, feel, and do, what you love—is the sum of what you focus on."

- Cal Newport

**"The Four Agreements:
1. Be impeccable with your word.
2. Don't take anything personally.
3. Don't make assumptions.
4. Always do your best."**

- Don Miguel Ruiz

"The real risk is doing nothing."

- Dennis Waitley

"Progress is impossible without change, and those who cannot change their minds cannot change anything."

- George Bernard Shaw

"Five percent of the people think;

ten percent of the people think they think;

and the other eighty-five percent would rather die than think."

- Thomas A. Edison

"Being attracted to someone's looks is one thing.

But being attracted to someone's:

-way of thinking

-healthy habits

-loyalty + honesty

-inner peace + self esteem

-generosity + kindness

-ability to give and receive love

Is a whole different level of attraction."

- Lewis Howes

"You can have everything in life that you want, if you'll just help enough other people get what they want."

- Zig Ziglar

"Goals are like magnets. They'll attract the things that make them come true."

- Tony Robbins

"The way to get started is to quit talking and begin doing."

- Walt Disney

"The only way to achieve greatness in life is to have patience, consistency, and discipline."

- David Goggins

"A wise man can learn more from a foolish question than a fool can learn from a wise answer."

- Bruce Lee

"Accept yourself, and keep moving forward. If you want to fly, you have to give up what weighs you down."

- Roy T. Bennett

"Do it now, sometimes later becomes never."

- Anonymous

"There are two great days in a person's life—the day we are born and the day we discover why."

- William Barclay

"To live is to suffer, to survive is to find some meaning in the suffering."

- Friedrich Nietzsche

"My goal is no longer to get more done, but rather to have less to do."

- Francine Jay

"Stop thinking, and end your problems."

- Lao Tzu

"When life knocks you around, look for the lesson. And never let go of the belief that you are capable of achieving your dreams."

- James Melouney

"Only put off until tomorrow what you are willing to die having left undone."

- Pablo Picasso

"Discipline is choosing between what you want now and what you want most."

- Abraham Lincoln

"If there's something that I want to do, but somehow can't get myself to do, it's because I don't have clarity."

- Gretchen Rubin

"Nothing we learn in this world is ever wasted."

\- Eleanor Roosevelt

"Success is about what you become, not what you get."

- James Melouney

"And if you think tough men are dangerous, wait until you see what weak men are capable of."

- Jordan B. Peterson

"Champions aren't made in the gyms. Champions are made from something they have deep inside them—a desire, a dream, a vision."

- Muhammad Ali

"The reason most people fail instead of succeed is they trade what they want at the moment."

- Napoleon Bonaparte

"I will no longer allow anyone to manipulate my mind and control my life in the name of love."

- Miguel Ruiz

"If you don't have ideas, read.

If you have ideas, but can't articulate them, write.

If you have ideas, and have the clarity to execute, build."

- Dan Koe

"Nothing great in the world has ever been accomplished without passion."

- Friedrich Hegel

"Critical thinking and curiosity are the key to creativity."

- Amala Akkineni

"If you don't produce, you won't thrive—no matter how skilled or talented you are."

- Cal Newport

"You never change your life until you step out of your comfort zone, change begins at the end of your comfort zone."

- Roy T. Bennett

"Repetition is the mother of learning, the father of action, which makes it the architect of accomplishment."

- Zig Ziglar

"You are the only person who can give yourself what you want."

- Lewis Howes

"A certain darkness is needed to see the stars."

- Osho

"If you want happiness for an hour, take a nap. If you want happiness for a day go fishing. If you want happiness for a year, inherit a fortune. If you want happiness for a lifetime, help somebody."

- Chinese Proverb

"Accept what is, let go of what was, and make changes toward what will be. Life's about taking action."

\- Kristen Butler

"Man is born free, but is everywhere in chains."

- Jean-Jacques Rousseau

"Day by day, what you think and what you do is who you become."

- Heraclitus

"All truly great thoughts are conceived while walking."

- Friedrich Nietzsche

"Treasure the love you receive above all. It will survive long after your good health has vanished."

- Og Mandino

"Only you can take inner freedom away from yourself, or give it to yourself. Nobody else can."

- Michael A. Singer

"If you're serious about changing your life, you'll find a way. If you're not, you'll find an excuse."

- Jen Sincero

"Whenever you do a thing, act as if all the world were watching."

- Thomas Jefferson

"Judge a man by his questions rather than by his answers."

- Voltaire

"The most difficult thing in life is to know yourself."

- Thales

"Distance yourself from the people that you don't want to become."

- Shane Parrish

"You have power over your mind not outside events. Realize this, and you will find strength."

- Marcus Aurelius

"Time management is about life management."

- Idowu Koyenikan

"People don't buy what you do; they buy why you do it. And what you do simply proves what you believe."

- Simon Sinek

"Never forget why you're really doing what you're doing. Are you helping people? Are they happy? Are you happy? Are you profitable? Isn't that enough?"

- Derek Sivers

"What we choose to focus on and what we choose to ignore—plays in defining the quality of our life."

- Cal Newport

"You are in danger of living a life so comfortable and soft, that you will die without ever realizing your true potential."

- David Goggins

"We are addicted to our thoughts. We cannot change anything if we cannot change our thinking."

- Santosh Kalwar

"Nothing we learn in this world is ever wasted."

- Eleanor Roosevelt

"To improve is to change, to be perfect is to change often."

- Winston Churchill

"The starting point in all achievement is desire."

- Napoleon Hill

"Enjoy the little things, for one day you may look back and realize they were the big things."

- Robert Brault

"Motivation is what gets you started, habit is what keeps you going."

- Jim Rohn

"The mind in it's own place, and in itself can make a heaven of hell, a hell of heaven."

- John Milton

"You were seen, you were heard, and you matter."

- Oprah Winfrey

"The key to success is to start before you are ready."

- Marie Forleo

"You must expect great things of yourself before you can do them."

- Michael Jordan

"If you set your goals ridiculously high and it's a failure, you will fail above everyone else's success."

- James Cameron

"If you don't have money, invest your time and energy until you do."

- Dan koe

"Change. But start slowly, because direction is more important than speed."

- Paulo Coelho

"There is no reason not to follow your heart."

- Steve Jobs

"Our bodies change our minds, our minds change our behaviour, and our behaviour changes our outcomes."

- Amy Cuddy

"Change might not be fast and it isn't always easy. But with time and effort, almost any habit can be reshaped."

- Charles Duhigg

"Whatever happens around you, don't take it personally. Nothing other people do is because of you. It is because of themselves."

- Don Miguel Ruiz

"If you are positive, you'll see opportunities instead of obstacles."

- Confucius

"You become what you think about all day long."

- Ralph Waldo Emerson

"The measure of intelligence is the ability to change."

- Albert Einstein

"To be a great champion, you must believe you are the best. If you're not, pretend you are."

- Muhammad Ali

"Success is no accident. It is hard work, perseverance, learning, studying, sacrifice and most of all, love of what you are doing or learning to do."

- Pele

"Try not to become a man of success. Rather become a man of value."

- Albert Einstein

"People who say it cannot be done should not interrupt those who are doing it."

- George Bernard Shaw

"Start where you are. Use what you have. Do what you can."

- Arthur Ashe

"One secret of success in life is for a man to be ready for his opportunity when it comes."

- Benjamin Disraeli

"You've got to get up every morning with determination if you're going to go to bed with satisfaction."

- George Lorimer

"Education is the most powerful weapon which you can use to change the world."

- Nelson Mandela

"When I believe in something, I'm like a dog with a bone."

- Melissa McCarthy

"Perfection is not attainable. But if we chase perfection we can catch excellence."

- Vince Lombardi

15481444R00066